Fluent Reader titles are ideal for children who can confidently read books with a wider vocabulary, and who are beginning to read longer stories by themselves.

Special features:

Full exploration of subject

Richer, more varied vocabulary

Detailed illustrations capture the imagination

Longer sentences

Captions offer further explanation

Ladybird

Educational Consultants: Geraldine Taylor and James Clements
Book Banding Consultant: Kate Ruttle
Subject Consultant: Philip Parker

LADYBIRD BOOKS
UK | USA | Canada | Ireland | Australia
India | New Zealand | South Africa

Ladybird Books is part of the Penguin Random House group of companies
whose addresses can be found at global.penguinrandomhouse.com.

www.penguin.co.uk www.puffin.co.uk www.ladybird.co.uk

Penguin Random House UK

First published 2018
This edition published 2024
001

Written by Simon Mugford

Illustrations by Leesh Li

Printed in China

The authorized representative in the EEA is Penguin Random House Ireland,
Morrison Chambers, 32 Nassau Street, Dublin D02 YH68

A CIP catalogue record for this book is available from the British Library

ISBN: 978-0-241-56389-2

All correspondence to:
Ladybird Books
Penguin Random House Children's
One Embassy Gardens, 8 Viaduct Gardens, London SW11 7BW

FSC www.fsc.org MIX Paper from responsible sources FSC® C018179

Read It Yourself

Ancient and Imperial China

Written by Simon Mugford
Illustrated by Leesh Li

Contents

Timeline

This is the timeline of ancient and imperial China.

221 BCE
The first emperor

475–221 BCE
Warring States

214 BCE
Emperor Qin Shi Huang-di's Great Wall

206 BCE–220 CE
Han Dynasty
(Confucius's ideas were important here)

1912 CE
The last emperor

1368–1644 CE
Ming Dynasty

Warring States

Different family dynasties had ruled China as separate states for thousands of years. From about 475 BCE to 221 BCE, the states had many wars with each other.

This was the time of the Warring States in ancient China.

The first emperor

The ruler of the Qin kingdom was very powerful. After many wars, he ruled the separate states as one kingdom and became the first emperor.

Imperial China lasted for 2,000 years.

Emperor Qin Shi Huang-di was the first emperor of China. He ruled in the Qin Dynasty.

Different dynasties

China was ruled by different dynasties at different times.

Qin Dynasty

Emperor Qin Shi Huang-di's dynasty was the first to rule over all of ancient China.

Han Dynasty

The rulers of the Han Dynasty made imperial China very powerful.

Han Dynasty soldiers

Ming Dynasty

Chinese education and ideas became more important at this time.

The Great Wall

The different Chinese states built enormous walls to defend their kingdoms. Qin Shi Huang-di built one of the biggest walls, and joined other, older walls together, too.

The Great Wall of China

Most of the Great Wall we see today was built by the Ming Dynasty (1368–1644 CE). It is very old.

Building the wall

Thousands of soldiers and workers built the wall for Emperor Qin.

The people worked on the Great Wall on and off for more than 1,500 years.

The Terracotta Army

An enormous tomb was built for the first emperor.

700,000 people helped to build the Terracotta Army and the big tomb. The work took about 40 years.

In the tomb, thousands of model soldiers defended the Emperor after he died.

Each of the model soldiers looked different.

The great inventors

Many goods that we still have today were invented in China. Silk, porcelain, fireworks, paper, printing and the compass are all Chinese inventions, and there are many more.

silk

porcelain

fireworks

paper

printed books

compass

Making paper

Paper was invented in China in about 100 CE. The first paper was made from tree bark.

How paper was made

1. The bark is taken off the tree.

2. The bark is put in water.

3. The bark becomes a pulp.

4. A screen is put into the pulp.

5. The pulp on the screen becomes paper when it is dry.

6. The dry paper comes off the screen.

Printing and power

As the rulers in China had more printed books, they became more educated and had good ideas. With more educated rulers, China became more powerful.

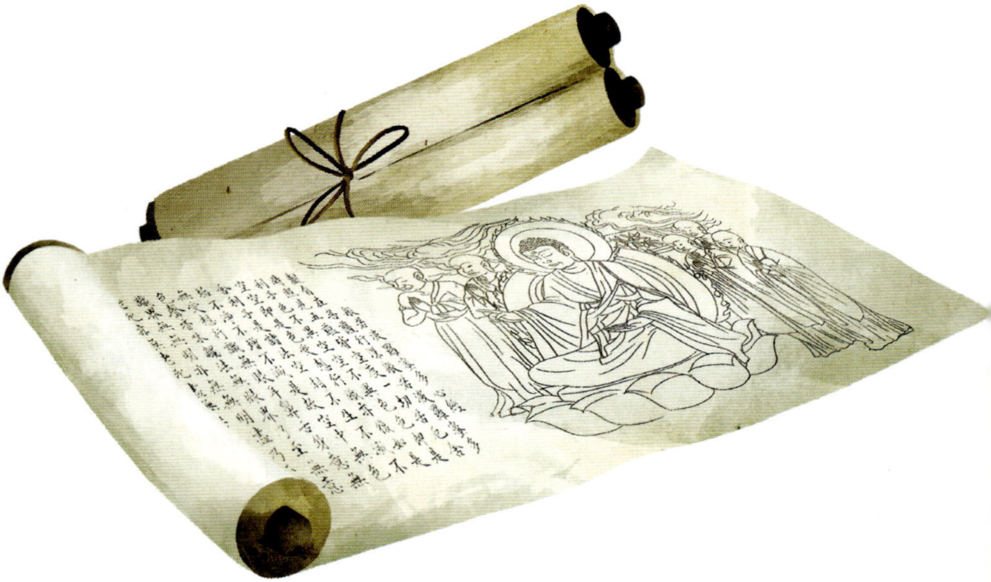

The world's first book was printed in China in 868 CE.

Chinese porcelain

The Chinese made the best porcelain in the world. The very best Chinese porcelain was made in the time of the Ming Dynasty.

How Ming porcelain was made

Porcelain like this has another name: “china”!

Chinese medicine

The Chinese have used herbs in medicine for over 4,000 years. They invented acupuncture, too. In acupuncture, needles are used to treat illness.

Chinese medicine and herbs are still used to treat illness today.

The Silk Road

The ancient Chinese were great traders. From about 200 BCE, they were trading silk and other goods with people to the west.

The way the traders went was named the "Silk Road".

The Silk Road brought new ideas
from China to the west, too.

The ideas of Confucius

Confucius lived before the time of the Warring States. He said that family was very important, and that people should treat each other well.

Confucius brought new ideas that helped make China great during the Han Dynasty.

Family life

In most Chinese families,
mum, dad, children
and grandparents
all lived together.

Family life had rules.
The grandparents were the most important people in the family, and were looked up to by the mum, dad, children and others.

Farming

Most people in ancient and imperial China lived by farming for food. The most important food in China was rice.

Families worked together
on farms. Rice is still
farmed in water, like this.

Chinese New Year

Chinese New Year has been celebrated for thousands of years. Today, it is an important time of year for Chinese people all over the world. Families come together to celebrate with food and fireworks.

People celebrate Chinese
New Year with fireworks!

China today

China is still a powerful and important country today, and Chinese goods are traded all over the world.

There are more people living in China than in any other country in the world.

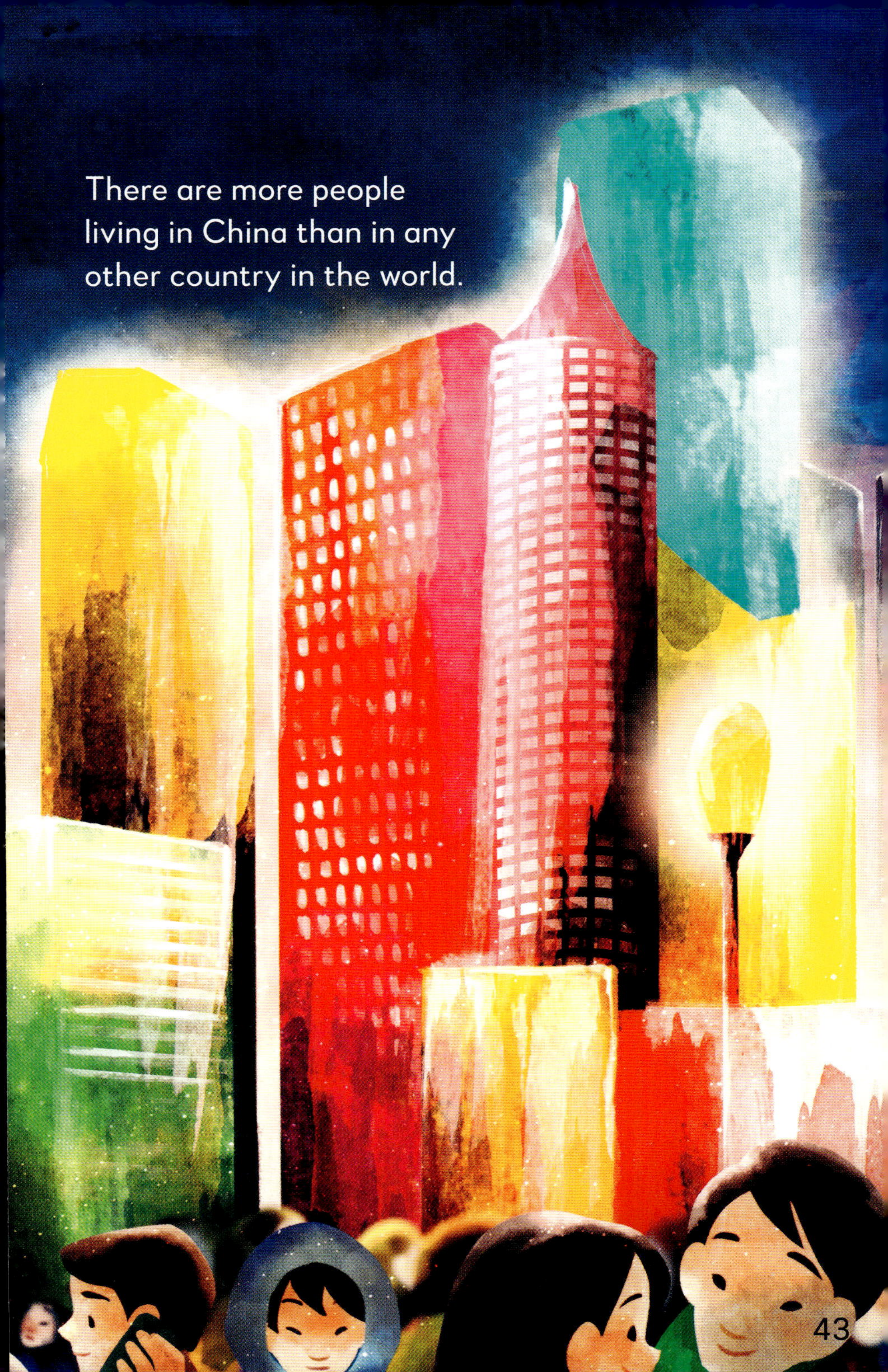

Picture glossary

compass

emperor

fireworks

Great Wall of China

medicine

paper

porcelain

printed books

rice farm

soldiers

Terracotta Army

tree bark

Index